Collins

Key Stage 3
Judaism

Andy Lewis
Series Editor: Robert Orme

T0340473

William Collins' dream of knowledge for all began with the publication of his first book in 1819. A self-educated mill worker, he not only enriched millions of lives, but also founded a flourishing publishing house. Today, staying true to this spirit, Collins books are packed with inspiration, innovation and practical expertise. They place you at the centre of a world of possibility and give you exactly what you need to explore it.

Collins. Freedom to teach

Published by Collins
An imprint of HarperCollins*Publishers*
The News Building
1 London Bridge Street
London SE1 9GF
HarperCollins *Publishers*
1st Floor
Watermarque Building
Ringsend Road
Dublin 4
Ireland

Text © Andy Lewis 2017
Design © HarperCollins*Publishers* 2017

10 9 8

ISBN 978-0-00-822771-5

A catalogue record for this book is available from the British Library

Publisher: Joanna Ramsay
Editor: Hannah Dove
Author: Andy Lewis
Series Editor: Robert Orme
Development Editor: Sonya Newland
Project Manager: Emily Hooton
Copy-editor: Jill Morris
Image researcher: Shelley Noronha
Proof-reader: Ros and Chris Davies
Cover designer: We Are Laura
Cover image: bogdan ionescu/Shutterstock
Production controller: Rachel Weaver
Typesetter: QBS
Printed and Bound in the UK using 100% Renewable Electricity at CPI Group (UK) Ltd

MIX
Paper from
responsible sources
FSC C007454

FSC is a non-profit international organisation established to promote the responsible management of the world's forests. Products carrying the FSC label are independently certified to assure consumers that they come from forests that are managed to meet the social, economic and ecological needs of present and future generations, and other controlled sources.

Find out more about HarperCollins and the environment at
www.harpercollins.co.uk/green

Contents

Introduction

It is not easy to define what makes something a religion. In some religions one god is worshipped, in others many gods are worshipped, and in some no god is worshipped at all. Some religions have a single founder. In others, there is not one person who starts it or one clear moment when it began. To make things more complicated, there are often strong differences of opinion between and even within particular religions. Two people following the same religion can believe opposing things and follow their religion in strikingly different ways. Within any religion, some people build their whole lives around their beliefs while others are less committed to their religion but still think of themselves as part of it. Followers of all religions believe that they have found truth, but their ideas about what is true differ greatly.

Approximately 84 per cent of people in the world today follow a religion and experts predict that this will rise to 87 per cent by 2050. The most followed religion in the UK is Christianity, but there are also followers of many other religions including Islam, Judaism, Buddhism, Hinduism and Sikhism. In recent times there has also been a big increase in the number of people in the UK who do not follow any religion. Some are atheists which means that they do not believe there is a god or gods. Others are agnostics meaning they are not sure if a god or gods exists. Others might believe there is a god or gods, but choose not to belong to a religion.

By studying the beliefs and ways of life of millions of people around the world, you will gain a greater understanding of the past, the modern world and humanity itself. You will explore questions that have troubled humankind through the ages and examine the diverse ways in which these questions have been answered. In a world where religion has and continues to play such a large role, the importance of understanding it is as great as ever.

Robert Orme (Series Editor)

Concise topic introductions set the scene and focus your learning.

Engaging photos illustrate the key ideas.

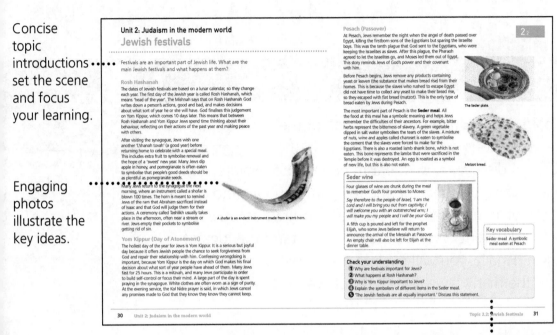

End-of-topic questions are designed to check and consolidate your understanding.

Key vocabulary lists for each unit help you define and remember important terms.

Key fact boxes help you to revise and remember the main points from each unit.

Key people boxes summarise the key figures from the unit.

Knowledge organisers can be used to revise and quiz yourself on key dates, definitions and descriptions.

History and belief

In this book, you will find out about one of the most influential and ancient religions on earth – Judaism. In the first half of the book, you will discover how Judaism began and explore some of the main ideas which shape the religion. You will find out why the city of Jerusalem is so important to Jews as well as examine the different ways that Jews understand the idea of the Messiah. Finally, you will explore how Jews worship, pray and follow the many laws that they believe God has given to them.

What is Judaism?

Judaism has played a significant role in human history, but when did it begin, and how does it continue to give significance to the lives of many millions of people?

Some religions begin with a single founder at a specific moment. Others develop gradually over a period of time. Jewish beliefs about how Judaism began are based on its most holy text, the **Torah**. According to the Torah, approximately 4000 years ago God made a **covenant** with a man called Abraham who lived in a city called Ur Kasdim, in what is now Iraq. God told Abraham that he had chosen him and his descendants to be a great nation of people who would have a special relationship with him.

Originally, the descendants of Abraham were known as Hebrews, or Israelites. People began to call them Jews about 2700 years ago. This was because many of them were living in a southern part of Israel called Judah. Today, Jews still believe that they are physical and spiritual descendants of Abraham, and that they have a special relationship or covenant with God.

Although Judaism is a very old religion, it is quite small. There are approximately 14 million Jews in the world, which is 0.2 per cent of the world's population. The country with the largest Jewish population is Israel, which is home to over 6 million Jews (75 per cent of the country's total population). There are also just under 6 million Jews in the USA and approximately 270,000 in the UK.

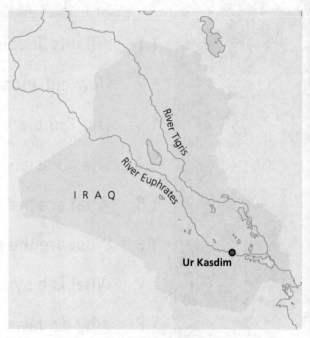

This map shows the location of Ur Kasdim, where Abraham is believed to have lived about 4000 years ago.

> **Fact**
>
> Jews meet to worship God in buildings called **synagogues**. The leader of a synagogue is called a **rabbi**, which means teacher.

What do Jews believe about God?

Jews are **monotheists**, which means they believe in one God. They consider God to be eternal, meaning he has no beginning or end, and that he is the creator of everything. Jews also believe that God is almighty – that he is very powerful – and that he is a good, loving God. Many Jews believe that the name of God is so holy that it should not be spoken or written. They often write 'G-d', or use names like 'Adonai' ('My Lord') or 'Hashem' ('The Name') instead.

What is the Tanakh?

The main Jewish scriptures are called the **Tanakh**, or sometimes the Hebrew Bible, because Hebrew is the language in which they were originally written. The Tanakh is divided into three sections. The most

Country	Jewish population
Israel	6,399,000
USA	5,300,000
France	465,000
Canada	385,000
UK	269,568
Russia	186,000
Argentina	181,000
Germany	99,695
Australia	112,500
Brazil	95,000

This table shows the 10 countries in the world with the highest population of Jews.

important is the Torah, which comes first. The Torah teaches Jews about how their religion began and the laws that God wants them to follow as part of their special covenant relationship. Jews tend not to be too focused on what happens after we die. Their focus is on living a good and holy life in the present. They believe that if they obey God's laws he will look after them.

Different types of Jews

Unlike many other religions, people are born into Judaism. Even if someone does not follow the religion, he or she may still be Jewish. Jews who do not believe in God are called **secular** Jews. Unlike some Christians and Muslims, Jews do not try to convert people to their religion. It is possible to convert to Judaism if there is a good reason, such as marriage, but the process can be long and difficult.

Orthodox Jews are one group of Jews. They believe it is essential to keep traditional beliefs and the Jewish way of life alive. Orthodox Jews think that the laws in the Torah show clearly how God wants Jews to live and should be closely followed. About half of Jews in Britain are Orthodox, and there are approximately 300 Orthodox synagogues. **Conservative Jews** are not as strict and traditional as Orthodox Jews. Although they preserve Jewish rituals and traditions, they are more flexible in interpreting Jewish laws in the modern world.

Hasidic Jews such as those in this image are part of Orthodox Judaism.

There are other groups of Jews known as **Reform Jews** and **Liberal Jews**. These two groups are different, but they share a view that Jewish belief and worship can change or modernise over time. For example, some Reform synagogues allow women to be rabbis, while Orthodox synagogues do not. Reform and Liberal Jews might also think that some of the laws in the Torah are not appropriate for today because they reflect the times in which they were written rather than how God wants people to live now.

Key vocabulary

Conservative Jews Jews who preserve Jewish rituals and traditions but are more flexible in interpreting Jewish laws than Orthodox Jews

covenant An agreement between God and people

Liberal Jews A group of Jews who believe that Judaism can change or modernise over time

monotheist Someone who believes in just one God

Orthodox Jews Jews who believe in maintaining the traditional beliefs and practices of Judaism and the laws given by God

rabbi The leader of a synagogue

Reform Jews A group of Jews who believe that Judaism can change or modernise over time

secular Non-religious

synagogue The Jewish place of worship

Tanakh The main Jewish scripture, which includes the Torah

Torah The most important holy text for Jews

Check your understanding

1 How did Judaism begin?
2 How many Jews are there in the world today?
3 Explain what Jews believe about God.
4 What is the Tanakh?
5 Explain why there are different groups of Jews today.

Unit 1: History and belief
How did Judaism begin?

The story of Judaism begins with three men known as the patriarchs. Who were they, and what do Jews believe about them?

Jews believe that nearly 4000 years ago, in the Middle East, God chose a man named Abraham to begin a new religion based on the radical idea of worshipping one God. Abraham was the first patriarch (founding father of Judaism). The second patriarch was Abraham's son Isaac, and the third was Isaac's son and Abraham's grandson, Jacob. These three men are believed to be the physical and spiritual ancestors of all Jews.

Who was Abraham?

Abraham lived around 4000 years ago. At this time, most people were **polytheists** – they believed in many gods. They sacrificed animals and occasionally humans to try and please their gods. It was also common to worship **idols**. Originally, Abraham was a polytheist, but during his life he came to believe that there was only one God, who had created everything. This was a very different belief from the polytheistic ideas of people in the Middle East, as well as other ancient civilisations.

According to the Torah, God tested Abraham in ten different ways to see how strong his faith was. In the first test, God told Abraham to leave his home in Ur. This was a difficult thing for Abraham to do because he was living a good and happy life, but he agreed. God made a covenant with Abraham, saying he would bless him and make his family a great nation. God told Abraham that all of the males in Abraham's family must be **circumcised** in order to show this special relationship.

> ### Fact
>
> According to Jewish tradition, Abraham's father sold idols for a living, but Abraham destroyed these when he started to believe in one God.

Who was Isaac?

Abraham thought that his wife Sarah was too old to have a baby, so he had a son with his wife's servant, Hagar. Their son was called Ishmael. However, Sarah also fell pregnant and gave birth to a son, named Isaac. God tested Abraham again, telling him to take Isaac to a place called Mount Moriah and to kill him on a **sacrificial altar**. Although Abraham had waited a long time to have a child, he travelled to the mountain with Isaac, and showed that he was willing to obey God. Just as Abraham was about to plunge his knife into his son, an angel of the Lord appeared and stopped him. Abraham had passed God's test.

Abraham and his son Isaac climbing Mount Moriah.

Who was Jacob?

Isaac had twin sons, Jacob and Esau. Jacob had 12 of sons of his own. During Jacob's lifetime, there was a drought throughout the land, and so he travelled to Egypt with his large family. They settled in Egypt and lived happily there for many years. God changed Jacob's name to Israel and the families of his sons became known as the **Twelve Tribes of Israel**.

Who was Moses?

Abraham's descendant Moses is another important figure in Judaism. By the time of Moses, Jacob's descendants, the Israelites, were being forced to work for the Egyptians as slaves. God told Moses to free the Israelites and lead them to the land that God had promised them.

At first, the **Pharaoh** refused to let the Israelites go, so God sent 10 plagues to Egypt. The final plague was an angel of death that killed all the firstborn sons in Egypt, including Pharaoh's oldest son. After this, he agreed to free the slaves, and Moses led them through the desert to the Red Sea. When they reached the water, God parted it so that they could pass through. The Israelites lived in the desert for 40 years before they finally settled in the **Promised Land**. During this time, God gave Moses the Ten Commandments – ten laws that the Israelites had to follow – on Mount Sinai. They are still very important for Jews today.

Moses parting the Red Sea.

Fact

Abraham is an important person in Christianity and Islam as well as Judaism. These religions are sometimes called the Abrahamic or monotheistic faiths.

Key vocabulary

circumcision The removal of a baby boy's foreskin at the age of eight days in Judaism

idols Statues that are worshipped

Pharaoh An Egyptian king

polytheist Someone who believes in more than one god

Promised Land An area of land in the Middle East given to Jews by God

sacrificial altar A place where animals were killed as offerings to God

Twelve Tribes of Israel The families of the sons of Jacob

Check your understanding

1 Approximately when did Judaism begin?
2 Who were the patriarchs?
3 Describe the beliefs of people who lived in the Middle East 4000 years ago.
4 Describe the life of Abraham.
5 Why is Moses an important figure in Jewish history?

The Temple

What is the Temple and why is it so important to Jews?

Particular places often have a special significance to followers of different religions. The Western Wall in Jerusalem is the most important site in the world for Jews. It is the remaining wall of a place called the Temple, in which their ancestors worshipped.

The First Temple

According to the Tanakh, King David (who ruled about 3000 years ago) had wanted to build a Temple to house the **Ark of the Covenant**, but it was not constructed until the reign of his son, King Solomon. The Temple was the only place where certain rituals such as animal sacrifices were performed, and most Jews would try to visit at least once a year, even if this required days of travelling.

Destruction of Temple of Jerusalem by Emperor Titus.

The First Temple was attacked on several occasions and was finally destroyed by the Babylonians between 586 and 587 BCE. The Jews themselves were captured and forced to live outside their homeland under Babylonian rule. This is known as the **Babylonian exile**. During this time, the Ark of the Covenant was lost.

The Second Temple

The Babylonian exile lasted for 59 years. After this, the Jews returned to Jerusalem and rebuilt the Temple. Historians are not sure exactly what this Temple was like, but sources including the Christian New Testament, the **Mishnah** and the writings of a Jewish historian called Josephus give us some idea.

Jerusalem had a population of around 150,000 at this time, but during important Jewish festivals more than a million people might crowd into the city. Originally, the Second Temple was probably quite modest, but to cope with these crowds the Roman governor, Herod, extended it into a huge, wondrous building, sometimes called 'Herod's Temple'. Parts were made from

> ### Fact
>
> Non-Jews sometimes refer to the Western Wall as the 'Wailing Wall'. This name comes from a time when Jews were banned from the city apart from one day a year, when they were allowed to cry at the ruins. Many Jews consider this name to be offensive.

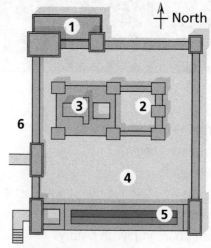

The Second Temple

1 Antonia Fortress
2 Inner Temple Precincts
3 Holy of holies
4 Court of the Gentiles
5 Royal Stoa
6 Western Wall

gold, and large bronze doors led to areas for making sacrifices, worship, socialising and studying.

At the centre of the Second Temple was the Holy of Holies, which was where the Ark of the Covenant had once been kept. With the Ark lost, this was left empty in the Second Temple. Only the High Priest was allowed in the Holy of Holies, and even then only on one special day of the year.

The Temple today

In 70 CE, the Temple was destroyed again, this time by the Romans. Today, the only part of the building that remains is a wall known as the Western Wall (*Kotel* in Hebrew). The earliest mentions of this as a place of **pilgrimage** for Jews are from the sixteenth century CE. Jews visiting the Western Wall often write prayers and put them into cracks between the stones.

A Jewish boy praying at the Western Wall.

The site of the Temple, including the Holy of Holies, is now occupied by Islamic buildings: the Dome of the Rock (a Muslim shrine) and the Al-Aqsa Mosque. Mosques are often built on holy sites, and Muslims believe that the Prophet Muhammad ascended into heaven from here. Since 1967, Jewish–Israeli authorities have had control of the Wall and the space in front of it, but over the past 100 years there has been much tension between Muslims and Jews in Jerusalem.

Rebuilding the Temple

In the fourth century CE, the Roman Emperor Julian began to have the Temple rebuilt. However, an earthquake brought work to a standstill, and the building was abandoned. Some Jews believe that the Temple will be rebuilt in the future and pray three times a day for this to happen, but some Jews reject the idea of rebuilding it. They believe that their synagogues are adequate places for worship and prayer.

Activity

Using the information on these pages, draw a timeline to show the history of the Temple in Jerusalem. If you can, find out more about it, and add some dates. You could illustrate it with suitable pictures from the internet.

Key vocabulary

Ark of the Covenant The box that housed the two tablets of stone on which the original Ten Commandments were written

Babylonian exile The period from 597 to 538 BCE when Jews were forced to live outside Jerusalem under Babylonian rule

Mishnah The early teachings of rabbis, which were passed on orally

pilgrimage A journey taken to a place of religious importance

Check your understanding

1. What was the First Temple built to house?
2. Why might some people refer to the Second Temple as 'Herod's Temple'?
3. When and by whom were the two Temples destroyed?
4. What is the Western Wall?
5. Why is the rebuilding of the Temple a controversial issue?

Unit 1: History and belief
The Messiah

What do Jews believe about the Messiah?

Originally, the term **Messiah** was used to describe a ceremony in which a man was anointed with holy olive oil and crowned as king. This act was done by a **prophet** or the **High Priest**. Later, Jews started using the word Messiah to mean a future king who would rule over them. According to the Tanakh, the Messiah would return Jews to Israel, bring peace, build the Third Temple and have a son who would be his heir. Some Jews are still waiting for this Messiah to come.

Jews believed that the Messiah would be a descendant of King David.

The Messianic Age

Some Jews believe that the arrival of the Messiah will be the start of a period of time known as the Messianic Age. According to the Tanakh, war will end, and all people will live in peace and harmony. It will be a time of freedom in which the covenants God made with the Jews will be restored forever. A book of the Tanakh called Micah has a verse (4.3) that describes this time:

> ❝ He will judge between many peoples and will settle disputes for strong nations far and wide. They will beat their swords into ploughshares and their spears into pruning hooks. Nation will not take up sword against nation, nor will they train for war any more. ❞

The 13 Principles of Faith

Orthodox Jews believe that they must uphold the 13 Principles of Faith, which were written by a rabbi called Maimonides in medieval times. One of these principles – number 12 – refers to the Messiah: 'I believe with perfect faith in the coming of the Messiah and even though he tarries, with all of that I await his arrival with every day.' This belief has helped sustain Jews through some of their darkest times. Many Jews executed by the Nazis during the Holocaust (see pages 38–39) recited these words as they went to their deaths.

Bar Kokhba means 'Son of the Star', which comes from a prophecy about the Messiah in the Hebrew Bible.

Has the Messiah come already?

Although the Christian Bible describes Jesus as a descendant of David, Jews do not believe that he was the Messiah. They do not think that he fulfilled the mission described in the Tanakh, nor do they believe that the Messiah will be divine, as Christians believe Jesus was.

Some Jews believed that a man called Shimeon ben Kosiba, known as Bar Kokhba, who lived about 100 years later than Jesus, more closely matched the description of the Messiah. He was a strong and charismatic leader who helped free Jerusalem from the Romans and restart worship and sacrifice at the site of the Temple. However, he was eventually killed by the Romans, and Jews decided that he was not the Messiah.

Modern Jewish views

Orthodox Jews believe that the Messianic Age will come in the future, as stated in the 13 Principles of Faith. Some Orthodox Jews, especially a group called **Hasidic Jews**, believe that there is one person in each generation who has the potential to be the Messiah and who will try to bring about the Messianic Age.

However, other Jews are reluctant to make any claims about the Messiah. They believe it is impossible to say what the Messianic Age will be like and allow individuals to make up their own minds. Many Reform Jews do not accept the idea of a Messiah, yet think the idea of a Messianic Age is a positive thing and that Jews should work towards a world where there is greater peace. Discussion of the Messiah does not play a big role in much of modern Judaism.

> ### Fact
>
> Hasidic Jews follow a strict religious lifestyle and have a distinctive appearance. They wear black clothes and do not cut the hair at the sides of their head (called payot) or their beards.

Hasidic Jewish men often wear a black hat and on special occasions some married men may wear a fur hat called a shtreimel.

> ### Key vocabulary
>
> **Hasidic Jews** A group within Orthodox Judaism who follow a strict religious lifestyle and have a distinctive appearance
>
> **High Priest** Historically, the highest rank of Jewish leader
>
> **Messiah** Anointed one
>
> **prophet** A messenger of God

Check your understanding

1. What does the word 'Messiah' mean?
2. Describe Jewish beliefs about the Messianic Age.
3. Why do Jews not believe that Jesus was the Messiah?
4. Who was Shimeon ben Kosiba and how did he match some of the descriptions of the Messiah?
5. Explain different modern Jewish perspectives on the Messiah.

What are the Tanakh and Talmud?

What are the most sacred texts for Jews, and why are they so important?

The Tanakh

Jewish scriptures are known as the Tanakh, or sometimes the Hebrew Bible. The Tanakh is divided into three sections:

- the Torah (the books of law)
- the Nevi'im (the books of the prophets)
- the Ketuvim (the books of writings).

The Torah

For Jews, the most important section of the Tanakh is the Torah. This contains five books: Genesis, Exodus, Leviticus, Numbers and Deuteronomy. The Torah explains the 'laws' that Jews must follow. In all, there are 613 laws, known as **mitzvot**. Some laws tell Jews how they should worship and what festivals they should observe. Others offer more general advice on how to live in ways that will please God.

The yad helps readers keep their place as they recite from the Torah.

Orthodox Jews try to keep as many of these mitzvot as possible. Conservative Jews will keep many, but may reinterpret some laws for modern life. However, Reform and Liberal Jews think that many of the laws are too difficult to keep, or are not relevant in the modern world. They believe that the Torah was not just revealed once, but is continuously being revealed to Jews. This means that how Jews lived in the past is not necessarily how they should live today.

In synagogues, a handwritten copy of the Torah is kept on a scroll. It is written in Hebrew, the language in which it was originally recorded. It is a great honour to be asked to read from the Torah in a synagogue, but to do so a Jew must first learn Hebrew. The person reading from the Torah uses a pointing stick with a hand on it called a **yad** so that no fingers damage the holy scroll. When it is not being used, the Torah is stored in the **Ark**.

The Nevi'im

The Nevi'im teaches Jews about the history of their religion as well as the words of their prophets. Jews believe that the prophets had special knowledge from God. This meant that they could tell people how God wanted them to behave, and sometimes they gave people strong warnings about their ways of life.

Parts of the Nevi'im are read during synagogue services, but they are usually read from a book rather than written on a scroll. Many parts of the Nevi'im are only read at home or for personal study.

The Ketuvim

The Ketuvim contains important stories from Jewish history. The section that Jews use most is the book of Psalms. This contains songs that praise God and make requests of him. They were written over a period of around 500 years by a number of authors, including King David and King Solomon. The psalms were first used by the Jews who worshipped in the Temple in Jerusalem.

The Talmud

The **Talmud** is a collection of teachings from rabbis compiled from around 200 to 500 CE, around 2500 years after the time of Abraham. It is made up of two parts, the Mishnah (the early teachings of rabbis, which were passed on orally) and the **Gemara**, a commentary on the Mishnah. These give lots of additional detail about the laws in the Torah, helping explain them so that Jews know how to live. The Talmud is sometimes referred to as the 'Oral Tradition' because the teachings were originally passed from rabbi to rabbi by word of mouth.

The Talmud.

Other writings

Other important writings for Jews include the **Midrash**, which includes rabbis' interpretations of and further information about the Torah, Jewish law and moral issues. There are also books of response, 'responsa', which are answers to questions focused on Jewish law. The world today is very different from the world in which Judaism began, so these are still being written to help Jews respond to the challenges of modern life that their ancestors did not face.

The Tishbi, a dictionary containing words used in the Talmud and Midrash.

Key vocabulary

Ark a cupboard in a synagogue where Torah scrolls are stored

Gemara Part of the Talmud, a commentary on the Mishnah

Midrash Jewish writings that include rabbis' interpretations of and further information about the Torah, Jewish law and moral issues

mitzvot Jewish laws (there are 613 in total); the singular is mitzvah

Talmud A collection of teachings from rabbis giving more information about the Torah

yad A pointer used to read the Torah in the synagogue

Check your understanding

1 What is the Tanakh?
2 Why is the Torah considered the most important collection of books for Jews?
3 What is the Talmud?
4 Explain how a Jew today might use each of the different books mentioned in this topic.
5 Why might the responsa help Jews today?

What are the mitzvot?

What laws do Jews live by and what do they believe about these laws?

There are 613 Jewish laws, known as mitzvot ('commandments' in Hebrew). These were given to Moses by God in order to teach Jews the best way to live. Those who follow the commandments will be rewarded and those who disobey them will be punished. We often think of rules as things that can cause difficulties, but Jewish scholars suggest that the mitzvot are a gift given to help Jews.

Study of the Torah including the mitzvot is an important part of life for Jews.

Interpretations of the mitzvot

Jews believe that they should follow the mitzvot because these laws have come from God and honouring them will deepen their relationship with him. Orthodox Jews believe that the Torah is the literal word of God, so the mitzvot should be followed at all times. This can present many challenges, particularly as some of the mitzvot mention the Temple in Jerusalem, which was destroyed nearly 2000 years ago.

Reform Jews have a different view. They believe that the mitzvot were from an ancient time and that not all of the laws are relevant today. They think it is acceptable to follow the mitzvot selectively and that God allows rabbis to reinterpret them for the modern world.

The mitzvot cover a wide range of topics. For example, they tell Jews that they should look after those in need and show acts of kindness. These acts may include visiting the sick, feeding the hungry or comforting mourners.

Jewish food laws

There are many food laws (**kashrut**) in Judaism. The Torah and Talmud both provide detailed guidance on how to keep these laws. Orthodox Jews try to observe all the rules of kashrut; Conservative Jews will keep many, but perhaps reinterpret some for the modern day. Reform and Liberal Jews will observe some of the laws.

Food that is acceptable to eat is described as **kosher**, which means 'fit' or 'correct'. Any food that is not kosher is described as **trefah** ('torn' in Hebrew). The Torah includes instructions about what food is acceptable and what is not. For example, eating pig meat is forbidden, and so most Jews will not eat pork. In order for meat to be kosher, the animal has to be killed by a kosher slaughterer. It is essential that this is done quickly, by making a deep cut in the animal's jugular vein (in the neck). Before the meat is eaten, all remaining blood must be drained from the meat.

Some scholars have suggested that in ancient times food laws had health benefits for Jews. For example, pigs carried diseases, so it made sense to not eat them. Also, not eating animals that were unconscious before being killed reduces the risk of eating an unhealthy animal.

> 66 26See, I am setting before you today a blessing and a curse – 27the blessing if you obey the commands of the Lord your God that I am giving you today; 28the curse if you disobey the commands of the Lord your God and turn from the way that I command you today by following other gods, which you have not known. 99
>
> Deuteronomy 11.26–28

Fact

If a Jewish person accidentally breaks kashrut, he or she might try to make amends by giving to charity, fasting or praying to God.

Mixing meat and dairy

The Torah states that some combinations of food are not acceptable. In Exodus 23.19 it says 'Do not cook a young goat in its mother's milk,' so Jews do not eat meat and dairy products at the same time. After eating meat, they usually wait either three or six hours before eating dairy. This means that a cheeseburger or a chicken curry containing cream would be trefah. However, a curry made with coconut milk would be kosher. After eating meat, a Jew would wait before having a milkshake or a cup of tea containing milk.

Orthodox Jews will usually have separate cutlery and crockery for meat and dairy products and if possible two sinks in their kitchen. Jewish food laws can cause problems when eating out – cooking methods as well as the food have to be kosher. This means that some Jews choose to eat out only in kosher restaurants. Usually, kosher restaurants are either dairy or meat restaurants. In a meat restaurant, the deserts will not include dairy products; for example, they may replace butter with margarine, which is made with oil.

> ❝ Any animal that has divided hoofs and is cleft-footed and chews the cud – such you may eat. ❞
> Leviticus 11.3

A kosher restaurant in Paris.

Some kosher symbols that are found on food.

Activity

Draw up a table with two columns. On one side list types of food and drink that are considered kosher and on the other types that are trefah. Try to include a variety of foods such different meats, fish and cheese.

Key vocabulary

kashrut Jewish food laws

kosher Food that is acceptable for Jews to eat; the word literally means 'fit'

trefah Food that Jews are forbidden to eat

Check your understanding

1. What is the origin of the mitzvot?
2. Why do Jews follow the mitzvot?
3. How do groups of Jews differ in their views about mitzvot?
4. Explain the kashrut that Jews follow.
5. 'Jewish food laws are outdated and irrelevant.' Discuss this statement.

Unit 1: History and belief
What is a synagogue?

Where do Jews go to worship and what happens during their religious services?

Jews worship in a synagogue, a word that means 'bringing together'. This is a fitting name, because Jews meet here as a community in order to learn about their ancestors and think about how God wants them to live. The connection between Jews and their family and friends throughout history is a very important part of the religion.

The Ark

The most important part of every synagogue is the Ark. This is a cupboard where the Torah is kept. The Ark is usually built into a wall that faces Jerusalem. This reminds Jews of the Holy of Holies in the Temple, where the Ark of the Covenant was stored. Above the Ark is the **ner tamid**, which means 'eternal light'. This is a light that is kept burning above or in front of the Ark at all times. It reflects God's eternal nature and the idea that the Jewish family will be everlasting. It also reminds Jews of the **menorah** that burned in the Temple.

The bimah

As well as an Ark, synagogues always have a **bimah** – a raised platform where the rabbi stands when leading the service. During a service, the Torah scrolls are taken from the Ark to the bimah and read from there. The **congregation** sits below the bimah, symbolising how the Torah is higher than humans. The design of synagogues reflects the Temple in Jerusalem, and the bimah represents the sacrificial altar.

In an Orthodox synagogue, women usually sit separately from men, as they did in the Temple. This is generally at the back of the synagogue or on a balcony. They may sit separately in Conservative synagogues too. In Reform and Liberal synagogues everyone sits together.

As well as a rabbi, who leads the service, there is often a cantor, who leads the music and singing. In Orthodox synagogues the cantor must be a man, but in Conservative, Liberal and Reform synagogues it may be a woman.

Conservative, Liberal and Reform synagogues also have female rabbis, but the vast majority of Orthodox communities do not. Members of the community may also help with parts of the service, for example, reading from the Torah. The main prayer book used in synagogues is called the **siddur**. It is written in Hebrew, but an English translation is also available in many synagogues.

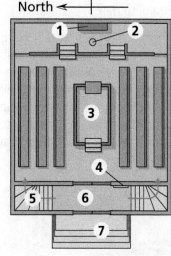

North ←

1 Ark containing the Torah
2 Ner tamid
3 Bimah
4 Memorial
5 Stairs up to women's gallery
6 Entrance hall and stairs
7 Porch

A plan of the inside of an Orthodox synagogue. Liberal or Reform Jews sometimes adapt buildings that were previously used for something else, and so their synagogues can have slightly different layouts.

The star of David is included on the flag of Israel.

The outside (and inside) of a synagogue may also be decorated with symbols. Two of the most important symbols in Judaism are the menorah and the star of David. The origins of the star of David are unknown, but it has been used for hundreds of years. The menorah symbolises divine light in the world. Some synagogues also have stained-glass windows like Christian churches and they sometimes contain artwork inside.

Famous synagogues

The oldest ruins of a synagogue were found on the Greek island of Delos. It is thought to have been built in around 150 BCE. The oldest synagogue in the world still in use is the Old New Synagogue of Prague in the Czech Republic, built in the 1270s. The Bevis Marks Synagogue is the oldest synagogue in the UK. It was built in London in 1701 and is the only synagogue in Europe to have held services continually for over 300 years.

One of the most famous synagogues in the world is the Hurva synagogue in Jerusalem. It has been destroyed on two occasions (1721 and 1948) and was most recently rebuilt in 2010.

Activity

In pairs, discuss why you think the synagogue is important for Jews.

Fact

Nobody is certain when Jews first started meeting in synagogues, but it was probably during the Babylonian exile. At this time Jews were living outside Jerusalem and could no longer worship in the Temple because it had been destroyed.

Key vocabulary

bimah The platform from where Torah scrolls are read

congregation People who attend a religious service

menorah A seven-branched candlestick and a symbol of divine light in the world

ner tamid The light in front of, or above, the Ark

siddur A Jewish prayer book

Check your understanding

1. What does the word 'synagogue' mean and why is this a fitting name?
2. Explain why some synagogues are different from others.
3. How might congregations be seated in different synagogues?
4. Who are the key people in a synagogue?
5. Describe the main features of a synagogue and explain what they are or what they symbolise.

Unit 1: History and belief
Why do Jews pray?

Prayer is an important part of Judaism, but how and why do Jews pray?

Many practising Jews pray three times a day: in the morning, afternoon and evening. Some Jews attend a synagogue every day for these prayers, but for most Jews this is not practical, so they will pray at home instead. Jews may also pray at many other times throughout the day.

There are many reasons why Jews pray. They may want to praise and thank God, to ask him for something or just to keep him at the forefront of their minds. Self-reflection is an important part of prayer for Jews and when Jews pray privately they usually do so silently. The main goal of all prayer is to build the relationship between the individual and God.

Dressed for prayer

While praying, men will usually cover their heads with a **kippah** to show respect to God. In some Jewish traditions, women also wear a kippah while they are praying. Men may wear a shawl called a **tallit**, which has 613 tassels to remind them of all the commandments in the Torah. By wrapping themselves in a tallit, Jews show that they wish to wrap themselves in God's will. Wearing it also helps them to focus on prayer. They may also strap two small boxes, called **tefillin**, to themselves, one to the forehead and the other on an arm. Each box contains verses from the Torah. They are worn to help focus the person's mind and heart on prayer.

An African Jew wearing a kippah.

Public prayer

Since the destruction of the Temple, daily prayers in local synagogues are seen as the most important act of Jewish worship. These prayers remind Jews that they are all part of an ancient community. In most synagogue services there are set prayers. These are written down so they can be recited by everyone together and are taken from the siddur.

In order for Jewish prayers to be recited and for the Torah to be read, there needs to be a minyan present. A minyan is a group of 10 people aged 13 or over. Praying together publicly helps create a sense of unity with both those present and the global Jewish community. This is because Jews know that others around the world are taking part in similar services and saying the same prayers as them. In an Orthodox synagogue, prayers will often be recited in Hebrew, but in other traditions of Judaism there is often a mixture of Hebrew and the local language.

A Jew in Israel wearing tefillin and a tallit.

The Shema

The most important prayer for Jews is called the **Shema**, which is a summary of what Jews believe. It is usually said twice a day – during morning and evening daily prayers. The Shema can often be found on doorposts in Jewish homes, in a small container called a **mezuzah**. When Judaism began, most people were polytheists. The Shema declares that there is only one God and that Jews should love him with their whole being and follow his laws. The first part is considered the most important, and is the part that is used most often:

Jews praying at the Western Wall.

Hear, O Israel, the Lord is our God, the Lord is One.
Blessed be the name of the glory of His kingdom forever and ever.
You shall love the Lord your God with all your heart, with all your soul, and with all your might. And these words which I command you today shall be upon your heart. You shall teach them thoroughly to your children, and you shall speak of them when you sit in your house and when you walk on the road, when you lie down and when you rise. You shall bind them as a sign upon your hand, and they shall be for a reminder between your eyes. And you shall write them upon the doorposts of your house and upon your gates.

Deuteronomy 6.4–9

Key vocabulary

kippah A head covering worn during prayer

mezuzah A small box attached to doorposts in Jewish homes, containing the Shema

Shema The most important prayer in Judaism

tallit A symbolic shawl worn during prayer

tefillin Two boxes worn during prayer, which contain verses from the Torah

A mezuzah.

Check your understanding

1 How often do most practising Jews pray?

2 Why do Jews pray?

3 Explain why praying in the synagogue is important for Jews.

4 Explain what the Shema could teach someone about Jewish beliefs.

5 'There is no point praying.' Discuss this statement, with reference to Judaism.

Knowledge organiser

Key vocabulary

Ark a cupboard in a synagogue where Torah scrolls are stored

Ark of the Covenant The box that housed the two tablets of stone on which the original Ten Commandments were written

Babylonian exile The period from 597 to 538 BCE when Jews were forced to live outside Jerusalem under Babylonian rule

bimah The platform from where Torah scrolls are read

circumcision The removal of a baby boy's foreskin at the age of eight days in Judaism

congregation People who attend a religious service

Conservative Jews Jews who preserve Jewish rituals and traditions but are more flexible in interpreting Jewish laws than Orthodox Jews

covenant An agreement between God and people

Gemara Part of the Talmud, a commentary on the Mishnah

Hasidic Jews A group within Orthodox Judaism who follow a strict religious lifestyle and have a distinctive appearance

High Priest Historically, the highest rank of Jewish leader

idols Statues that are worshipped

kashrut Jewish food laws

kippah A head covering worn during prayer

kosher Food that is acceptable for Jews to eat; the word literally means 'fit'

menorah A seven-branched candlestick and a symbol of divine light in the world

Messiah Anointed one

mezuzah A small box attached to doorposts in Jewish homes, containing the Shema

Midrash Jewish writings that include rabbis' interpretations of and further information about the Torah, Jewish law and moral issues

Mishnah The early teachings of rabbis, which were passed on orally

mitzvot Jewish laws (there are 613 in total); the singular is mitzvah

monotheist Someone who believes in just one God

ner tamid The light in front of, or above, the Ark

Orthodox Jews Jews who believe in maintaining the traditional beliefs and practices of Judaism and the laws given by God

Pharaoh An Egyptian king

pilgrimage A journey taken for religious reasons

Pilgrimage A journey taken to a place of religious importance

polytheist Someone who believes in more than one god

Promised Land An area of land in the Middle East given to Jews by God

prophet A messenger of God

rabbi The leader of a synagogue

Reform Jews and **Liberal Jews** Jews who believe that Judaism can change or modernise over time

sacrificial altar A place where animals were killed as offerings to God

secular Non-religious

Shema The most important prayer in Judaism

siddur A Jewish prayer book

synagogue The Jewish place of worship

tallit A symbolic shawl worn during prayer

Talmud A collection of teachings from rabbis giving more information about the Torah

Tanakh The main Jewish scripture, which includes the Torah

tefillin Two boxes worn during prayer, which contain verses from the Torah

Torah The most important holy text for Jews

trefah Food that Jews are forbidden to eat

Twelve Tribes of Israel The families of the sons of Jacob

yad A pointer used to read the Torah in the synagogue

Key facts

- The origins of Judaism go back about 4000 years, when God made a covenant with Abraham to make him leader of God's chosen people. They were known originally as Israelites, but were later called Jews.

- God tested Abraham's faith by asking him to sacrifice his son Isaac. Abraham was willing to do so and God spared Isaac.

- Jews view Abraham as the first patriarch. Isaac was the second patriarch and his son Jacob was the third. Moses is also an important figure for Jews.

- The Temple was the most important place for Jews. Built by King Solomon, it was destroyed by the Babylonians, but later rebuilt. The Romans destroyed the Second Temple. One wall remains, known as the Western Wall.

- There are different types of Jews, including Orthodox, Reform and Liberal Jews, who believe slightly different things and practise Judaism in different ways.

- Jews believe that the coming of a Messiah, or saviour, will mark the start of a new age when people will live in peace and harmony. Unlike Christians, Jews do not believe that Jesus was the Messiah.

- The two most important scriptures for Jews are the Torah (part of the Tanakh) and the Talmud (a collection of writings by rabbis).

- Jewish law is known as the mitzvot – a collection of 613 rules and instructions on how Jews should live their lives.

- There are strict laws about what Jews can eat. Permitted food is called kosher ('fit'). Food that is banned is known as trefah ('torn').

- Jews worship in buildings called synagogues. The most important part of the synagogue is the Ark – a special cupboard where the Torah is kept.

- When Jews pray, they may wear particular items of clothing that have special meaning: a kippah (head covering), tallit (shawl) and tefillin (two small boxes strapped to the forehead and arm).

Key people

Abraham A man who God made a covenant with that he would have many descendants who would be a great nation

Herod A Roman governor who built an extension to the Second Temple

Isaac The son of Abraham and the second patriarch

Jacob The son of Isaac and the third patriarch

Moses A man who received the laws including the Ten Commandments from God

Solomon The king of Israel who built the first Temple in Jerusalem

Jews praying together publicly.

Judaism in the modern world

The world today is very different from the way it was when Judaism began. Jews around the world now face challenges that people in the past did not have to consider. In the second half of this book you will see how Jews respond to these challenges and keep their faith strong. You will also discover how Judaism has survived extreme persecution over the course of its long history and explore how its followers have tried to make sense of the suffering that they have experienced. Finally, you will examine the role that Judaism plays in one of the most complex conflicts in the modern world. As you study more about Judaism, you will gain a greater understanding of the past, the modern world and the lives of millions of people around the world who call themselves Jews.

Unit 2: Judaism in the modern world
What is Shabbat?

Keeping the ancient tradition of **Shabbat** alive is an important part of following God's law and keeping the Jewish community strong. How do Jews do this?

A day of rest

Once a week, Jews stop their normal activities and have a day of rest. This is called Shabbat, or the **Sabbath**. Shabbat literally means 'ceasing'. Shabbat begins at sunset on Friday evening and ends one hour after sunset on Saturday evening. This means that the exact timings change throughout the year. Orthodox Jews use a special calendar that tells them when Shabbat should start and end. Some Reform Jews may choose to observe Shabbat from 6.00 p.m. on Friday to 6.00 p.m. on Saturday.

What are the origins of Shabbat?

The idea of Shabbat comes from the book of Genesis in the Torah, which says that God created the world in six days and rested on the seventh day. In the second book of the Torah, Exodus, Moses receives the Ten Commandments from God on Mount Sinai. The fourth commandment is to observe Shabbat. As such, keeping Shabbat is an important part of following God's law, and continues a tradition that dates back thousands of years. In the modern world different Jews observe Shabbat in different ways.

> ❝ Six days you shall labour and do all your work; but on the seventh day, which is a Sabbath in honour of the Lord your God, you shall not do any work. ❞
>
> Exodus 20.9–10

What counts as work?

The Torah describes 39 types of action as work, so these are all forbidden on Shabbat. If something is not mentioned, Jews will try to decide if it counts as work or not, but there is not always agreement. Orthodox Jews follow the rules about not working very strictly. They may switch off electronic devices such as mobile phones and will not use their car or even public transport. Because of this, Orthodox Jews often live within walking distance of the synagogue, where they spend Shabbat. Reform Jews often argue that it is more important to attend the synagogue than not drive a car. It is common for Reform Jews to refer to their rabbi for advice on what counts as work in the modern world.

Maintaining a strong community is an extremely important part of Judaism. Observing Shabbat every week helps keep the Jewish community connected and strong. It is a time to be with family, to socialise and relax, and to worship with other Jews in the synagogue. Some Jews also dedicate time to studying the Torah during Shabbat.

Hasidic Jews walking to the synagogue on a Saturday.

Shabbat at home

Before Shabbat, the family home is usually cleaned and tided. Sometimes flowers are put on display. All food is prepared before sunset on Friday because cooking is considered work. On the Friday evening, Jewish families have a special meal together. This begins with the father saying a special blessing over a cup of wine, called a Kiddush blessing. Kiddush means 'making holy'. The Kiddush cup is then passed around the table. Two portions of a special bread, called challah, are eaten at Shabbat meal. Before being eaten, the bread is blessed. At the end of Shabbat, blessings are recited over wine, spices and a candle.

Shabbat in the synagogue

There are usually two services in the synagogue during Shabbat. One is at sunset on the Friday; the other is on Saturday morning. Some Jews will attend both; others will attend one. The Saturday service can last up to two hours.

The challah bread reminds Jews of the food that God provided when they were in the desert during the Exodus.

A variety of things happen during this service. The first part of the Shema is recited as the Torah is removed from the Ark. The Torah is then read by someone from the bimah. In Reform synagogues, it is read in people's first language as well as Hebrew. The Torah is then returned to the Ark and a sermon is given by the rabbi (again in the language of the congregation). Following this, more prayers are said, including the 'Aleinu', which reminds Jews that it is their duty to praise God: 'Let us now praise the Sovereign of the universe and proclaim the greatness of the Creator…' This is followed by a prayer called the Kaddish, which says: 'Exalted and hallowed be God's great name, in the world which God created according to plan.' The service concludes with singing a hymn to God called 'Master of the World'.

Shabbat times on a smart phone.

> ### Activity
>
> Imagine you have spent Shabbat with a Jewish family. Describe what happened during the course of Shabbat.

> ### Key vocabulary
>
> **Shabbat/Sabbath** A day of rest and religious observance

Check your understanding

1 When do Jews observe Shabbat?

2 What are the origins of Shabbat?

3 How do Jews define work? Give examples of what might be considered work.

4 Why do you think it might be hard for Jews to observe Shabbat in the modern world?

5 'All Jews should observe Shabbat.' Discuss this statement.

Unit 2: Judaism in the modern world
Jewish festivals

Festivals are an important part of Jewish life. What are the main Jewish festivals and what happens at them?

Rosh Hashanah

The dates of Jewish festivals are based on a lunar calendar, so they change each year. The first day of the Jewish year is called Rosh Hashanah, which means 'head of the year'. The Mishnah says that on Rosh Hashanah God writes down a person's actions, good and bad, and makes decisions about what sort of year he or she will have. God finalises this judgement on Yom Kippur, which comes 10 days later. This means that between Rosh Hashanah and Yom Kippur Jews spend time thinking about their behaviour, reflecting on their actions of the past year and making peace with others.

After visiting the synagogue, Jews wish one another 'L'shanah tovah' (a good year) before returning home to celebrate with a special meal. This includes extra fruit to symbolise renewal and the hope of a 'sweet' new year. Many Jews dip apple in honey, and pomegranate is often eaten to symbolise that people's good deeds should be as plentiful as pomegranate seeds.

Many Jews return to the synagogue the next morning, where an instrument called a shofar is blown 100 times. The horn is meant to remind Jews of the ram that Abraham sacrificed instead of Isaac and that God will judge them for their actions. A ceremony called Tashlikh usually takes place in the afternoon, often near a stream or river. Jews empty their pockets to symbolise getting rid of sin.

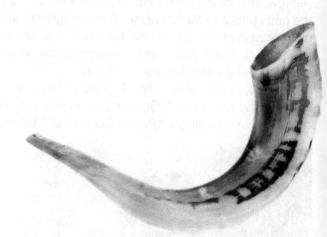

A shofar is an ancient instrument made from a ram's horn.

Yom Kippur (Day of Atonement)

The holiest day of the year for Jews is Yom Kippur. It is a serious but joyful day because it offers Jewish people the chance to seek forgiveness from God and repair their relationship with him. Confessing wrongdoing is important, because Yom Kippur is the day on which God makes his final decision about what sort of year people have ahead of them. Many Jews fast for 25 hours. This is a mitzvah, and many Jews participate in order to build self-control or focus their mind. A large part of the day is spent praying in the synagogue. White clothes are often worn as a sign of purity. At the evening service, the Kol Nidre prayer is said, in which Jews cancel any promises made to God that they know they know they cannot keep.

Pesach (Passover)

At Pesach, Jews remember the night when the angel of death passed over Egypt, killing the firstborn sons of the Egyptians but sparing the Israelite boys. This was the tenth plague that God sent to the Egyptians, who were keeping the Israelites as slaves. After this plague, the Pharaoh agreed to let the Israelites go, and Moses led them out of Egypt. This story reminds Jews of God's power and their covenant with him.

Before Pesach begins, Jews remove any products containing yeast or leaven (the substance that makes bread rise) from their homes. This is because the slaves who rushed to escape Egypt did not have time to collect any yeast to make their bread rise, so they escaped with flat bread (matzot). This is the only type of bread eaten by Jews during Pesach.

The Seder plate.

The most important part of Pesach is the **Seder meal**. All the food at this meal has a symbolic meaning and helps Jews remember the difficulties of their ancestors. For example, bitter herbs represent the bitterness of slavery. A green vegetable dipped in salt water symbolises the tears of the slaves. A mixture of nuts, wine and apples called charoset is eaten to symbolise the cement that the slaves were forced to make for the Egyptians. There is also a roasted lamb shank bone, which is not eaten. This bone represents the lambs that were sacrificed in the Temple before it was destroyed. An egg is roasted as a symbol of new life, but this is also not eaten.

Matzot bread.

Seder wine

Four glasses of wine are drunk during the meal to remember God's four promises to Moses:

Say therefore to the people of Israel, 'I am the Lord and I will bring you out from captivity; I will welcome you with an outstretched arm; I will make you my people and I will be your God.

A fifth cup is poured and left for the prophet Elijah, who some Jews believe will return to announce the arrival of the Messiah at Passover. An empty chair will also be left for Elijah at the dinner table.

Key vocabulary

Seder meal A symbolic meal eaten at Pesach

Check your understanding

1. Why are festivals important for Jews?
2. What happens at Rosh Hashanah?
3. Why is Yom Kippur important to Jews?
4. Explain the symbolism of different items in the Seder meal.
5. 'The Jewish festivals are all equally important.' Discuss this statement.

Unit 2: Judaism in the modern world
Birth, Bar Mitzvah and Bat Mitzvah

Important moments in the life of a Jew are marked by ancient rituals that are part of Jewish law. What are these moments and how are they honoured?

Birth

Jews believe that before a baby is born it has a soul, but its life does not begin until it has half emerged from its mother's body. When a baby is born it is sinless and pure. It is seen as a gift from God that should be celebrated.

In ancient times a woman had to spend time away from the Temple after giving birth. She was not permitted to touch anything sacred. This lasted for 40 days if the baby was a boy and 80 days if it was a girl, because the mother had created another creator. After this time, the woman would go to the Temple and make an offering to God. This ritual was based on the teachings of Leviticus 12 in the Torah. Today, a Jewish woman will have a mikvah (ritual bath) after a minimum period of 7 days if she has given birth to a boy and 14 days for a girl.

Circumcision

Circumcision is when a boy's foreskin is removed. This ceremony is performed when the baby is eight days old. In the past, fathers would often circumcise their sons, but today it is normally done by someone who is both religiously and medically qualified, called a **mohel**.

Circumcision is one of the most observed mitzvot. Even many secular Jews circumcise their sons. It is an ancient ritual, dating back to Abraham: God told the patriarch that he must circumcise himself and his descendants as a sign of God's everlasting covenant.

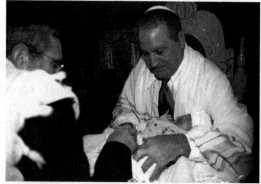

A father and his newborn son in a Jewish circumcision ceremony.

Circumcision of baby boys is practised in both Judaism and Islam, but it is a controversial issue in the modern world. Some **atheists** argue that parents should not choose their son's religion before he is able to accept it for himself. They may also think it is wrong to make a permanent physical change to the body.

> ## Fact
>
> Many Jewish children are given two names. One is a Hebrew name; the other is a local name. A baby girl is given her names in the synagogue after her father has performed a special reading from the Torah. Boys are named after eight days, during their circumcision.

Bar Mitzvah and Bat Mitzvah

When boys and girls 'come of age' they have a ceremony called a **Bar Mitzvah** (boys) or **Bat Mitzvah** (girls). In Reform and Liberal communities, this happens at the age of 13. In Orthodox synagogues, girls usually have it a year earlier, at the age of 12. After the ceremonies, the young person is considered to be responsible for his or her own actions and faith. After the Bar Mitzvah, the boy can lead the synagogue service, can be included in a minyan or read from the Torah in the synagogue. In a Reform or Liberal synagogue, these rights would also be given to a girl after her Bat Mitzvah. After the ceremony, the boy will also begin to wear the tefillin in the synagogue. Some Liberal synagogues have a further service when the young person reaches 15 or 16, in which he or she confirms acceptance of the Jewish way of life.

For each ceremony, Jews are expected to study and prepare carefully, and they have to read certain texts. Most boys read from the Torah during their Bar Mitzvah, so they must have a basic understanding of Hebrew and how to read it. Girls will also spend time learning, volunteering and doing charitable tasks. Often their mother will teach them how to make challah bread for Shabbat. This emphasises the importance of the home to the Jewish way of life. In Reform and Liberal communities, it is common for boys to also be taught about jobs in the home, and girls will also read from the Torah at their Bat Mitzvah.

After the Bar or Bat Mitzvah ceremony has taken place in the synagogue, a special meal is shared. This is often followed by a celebratory event with family, friends and the synagogue community.

Fact

In Hebrew, Bar Mitzvah literally means 'son of the commandments' and Bat Mitzvah means 'daughter of the commandments'. There are references to the Bar Mitzvah in the Talmud, but the Bat Mitzvah has only been celebrated during the last century of Judaism.

Key vocabulary

atheist Someone who does not believe in God

Bar Mitzvah A ceremony for boys at the age of 13; it literally means 'son of the commandments'

Bat Mitzvah A ceremony for girls at the age of 12 or 13; it literally means 'daughter of the commandments'

mohel Someone who is both medically and religiously qualified to perform a circumcision

Check your understanding

1 What do Jews believe about newborn babies?
2 Describe what happened to the woman after giving birth in the times of the Temple and what happens today.
3 Why are Jewish boys circumcised?
4 Explain the key differences between Orthodox and Reform/Liberal Bar and Bat Mitzvahs.
5 'The Bar/Bat Mitzvah is the most important moment in the life of a Jew.' Discuss this statement.

Unit 2: Judaism in the modern world
Marriage, funerals and mourning

What rituals do Jews perform during marriage and funeral ceremonies, and how do these help create a unique identity for Jews?

Marriage

The Torah does not provide Jews with much guidance about marriage. However, the Talmud explains how to find a partner, how a wedding ceremony should be conducted and how a husband and wife should treat each other. There are two stages to a Jewish marriage:

- kiddushin – the engagement between the couple

- nisuin – the full marriage.

A Jewish wedding ceremony usually lasts about half an hour. During the ceremony, the couple stands under a canopy called a **huppah**, which represents their new home together. The rabbi gives a talk, offering the couple a message about married life. The rabbi and guests also recite the **seven blessings** they hope that the couple will receive from God. In accordance with Jewish law, a plain metal ring is placed on the bride's right forefinger to show that the marriage has taken place.

In Orthodox ceremonies, the wedding and signing of the marriage contract has to be witnessed by two men. In other Jewish traditions, the witnesses can be men or women. After the signing of the contract, the groom stamps on a small glass as a reminder of the destruction of the Temple. After the ceremony, the couple retires to a room so they can spend some time alone before they re-join their family and friends for a meal and party.

The groom at a Jewish wedding ceremony sipping the wine which is blessed with the seven blessings.

Fact

In medieval times, some Jews believed in reincarnation – that your soul is reborn into another body after you die. Nowadays, Jews tend not to believe that souls are reincarnated.

Funerals

Some Reform and Liberal communities allow the bodies of dead people to be cremated, but, traditionally, the bodies of Jewish people are buried. In some countries, the body may simply be covered in a cloth, but in others Jews will usually use a very simple wooden coffin. If possible, the burial takes place within 24 hours of death, and the body is never left alone between the point at which a person dies and the burial. During this time, family members and friends pay respect to the person who has died. The body will be washed and wrapped in a shroud, and a tallit will be put on men. Some funerals take place in a synagogue, but others may be held at a funeral home or at the graveside. Services usually include readings, singing psalms and giving a **eulogy**.

Orthodox Jews paying respect at a Jewish funeral.

Mourning

When a loved one dies, people sometimes spend time mourning before returning to normal life. Mourning is an important part of Jewish life and this period follows five stages:

- Aninut – death to burial

- Shivah – the first seven days, starting on the day of burial

- Sheloshim – the first 30 days, starting on the day of burial and including the Shivah; this is the end of mourning, except when mourning for a parent

- Yud Bet Chodesh – the 'year of mourning' for a parent

- Yahrzeit – the anniversary of the death of the parent, according to the Jewish calendar

Orthodox Jewish prayer recited to honour the passing of a loved one, celebrate their life and help with coping during the mourning process.

Jews who are mourning might wear a torn black ribbon or a cut tie. This is because in the Torah, Jacob tore his clothes after hearing that his son Joseph had died. After the funeral, the mourners return home, and often share a meal of consolation. Stones are usually left at the grave rather than flowers. This is partly because stones are a permanent reminder and because stones were used to mark graves in the area where Judaism developed.

The seven days after the burial are a time for intense mourning during which Jews often stay at home, rejecting luxuries and fun activities. Special candles are lit and visitors will come to pay their respects, bringing food.

Life after death

Judaism focuses on this life rather than the next, so Jews have many different opinions about what happens after death. Some Jews speak about Olam Ha-Ba, which means 'the world to come', and Jews are generally convinced that death is not the end. Some believe there will be judgement and that those who follow God's commands will be welcomed to a place of spiritual perfection called Gan Eden; those who do not will go to **Gehinnom**, a place of purification. There is very little in the Tanakh about what happens when people die and most teaching about life after death comes from ancient rabbis.

> ## Key vocabulary
>
> **eulogy** A speech given in praise of someone who has just died
>
> **Gehinnom** A place of purification in the afterlife
>
> **huppah** A canopy which a couple stand under during their marriage ceremony to represent starting a new home together
>
> **seven blessings** Blessings recited by the rabbi and others at a wedding ceremony

---

Check your understanding

1 What are the two stages to a Jewish marriage?

2 Outline what happens at a Jewish wedding ceremony.

3 Create a timeline of events from the death of a Jew to the end of mourning.

4 What do Jews believe about life after death?

5 'It is better to focus on this life than what might happen next.' Discuss this statement, with reference to Judaism.

The value of human life

Obeying God's laws (mitzvot) is very important to Jews. What do Jews believe about human life?

Jews believe that the life of a human is more valuable than the life of any other living creature. They think that life should be respected because it is given by God and so is sacred. The Talmud states that everyone is descended from a single person, so harming or destroying one person is in some way like destroying the whole world.

What is Pikuach Nefesh?

Pikuach Nefesh is the idea that nearly any religious law can be broken in order to preserve human life. Jews believe that they should live by the Torah, but not die because of it. This means that if someone's life would be put in risk by fasting at Yom Kippur then the person should not fast. Equally, if someone is in danger of starvation, then it is acceptable to eat non-kosher food.

In the same way, it is acceptable to work on Shabbat if doing so will save someone's life. For example, doctors are allowed to answer emergency calls, and people can travel to hospitals in an emergency, even though driving is usually considered work. The principle of Pikuach Nefesh does not simply allow people to break laws – it actually requires that laws are broken in some situations. Leviticus 19.16 says 'You shall not stand aside while your fellow's blood is shed' and the Talmud says 'The Sabbath has been given to you, not you to the Sabbath.'

However, there are exceptions to the principle of Pikuach Nefesh. For example, adultery, murder, idolatry, denying God exists or using his name in vain should never be committed in order to save a life. Also, people should not put their own life in more danger than the person whose life they are trying to save.

Medical issues

The principle of Pikuach Nefesh also affects Jewish attitudes to abortion. Jews believe that if a pregnant woman is going to die, but having an abortion would save her life, then the foetus should be aborted. This is because her life is superior to the life of the foetus, which is not yet a human. Jews may think that it is acceptable to switch off life-support machines, but generally they think it is wrong to do anything that will bring about death.

One way in which people can help save lives is through donating their organs after they die. Liberal and Reform Jews usually allow organ donation. However, Orthodox Jews do not always agree with this, because sometimes the organs need to be removed while the donor's heart is still beating, which could be seen as killing that person.

Mount Sinai Hospital in the USA has a specially designed 'Shabbat elevator' that stops on every floor so that people observing Shabbat do not have to push a button in the lift, which would count as work.

Tattoos and piercings

Recently, tattoos and piercings have become more popular in society, and whether or not these are permitted has caused controversy among Jews. Many Jews think that these are banned in the Torah, which says: 'Do not cut your bodies for the dead or put tattoo marks on yourselves' (Leviticus 19.28).

Jews believe that our bodies are created in the image of God and should be seen as a precious gift, loaned from him. This means they are not our personal property to do with as we like. Piercing is less controversial because there are stories of Jews who have pierced ears in the Tanakh. Many Jews argue that a piercing is not a permanent act, and if ears can be pierced it is hard to justify other piercings being banned.

A Jewish man with a star of David tattoo.

Interpreting the Torah

The Torah teaches that people should be held accountable for their actions. A famous verse says: 'A life for a life, an eye for an eye, a tooth for a tooth' (Exodus 21.24).

It is unlikely that Jews ever took this verse literally. Often, justice would have been gained through payment of money to make up for a crime. The Talmud makes it clear that the Torah should not be taken literally and that it can only be fully understood with the Talmud's commentary. Jews believe that when someone has hurt another person, he or she should recognise this and seek forgiveness from God.

Key vocabulary

Pikuach Nefesh The principle that nearly any religious law can be broken in order to preserve human life

Check your understanding

1. Why do Jews believe that human life is sacred?
2. What does the principle of Pikuach Nefesh require of Jews?
3. Describe some modern situations where the principle of Pikuach Nefesh might be used.
4. Discuss different Jewish approaches to organ donation, tattoos or piercings.
5. How might Jews respond to the claim that they need to follow the teaching 'an eye for an eye' by seeking revenge?

Unit 2: Judaism in the modern world
A persecuted people

Through history, Jews have suffered for their beliefs. How and why have Jews been persecuted?

Early persecution

Jews have been **persecuted** since the early days of their religion. The book of Exodus describes how Moses freed the descendants of Abraham, the Israelites, from slavery in Egypt. The Tanakh also describes how the Jews lived under the control of the Babylonians after they invaded Jerusalem in 586 BCE and destroyed the Temple (see page 12). In 167 BCE, all Jewish worship, festivals and sacrifice were banned by the rulers of a Greek empire that took control of the area in which most lived. They forced Jews to worship Greek gods. In 70 CE, the Jewish Temple was destroyed for a second time, this time by the Romans who believed in many gods and did not like Jewish monotheism. This event caused Jewish communities to begin to spread around the world in an event called the diaspora ('dispersion').

The massacre of Jews in Rhineland, 1096.

Middle Ages

During the Middle Ages, some Christians blamed Jews for the death of Jesus, and **anti-Semitism** became common in Europe. Many Jews were murdered or expelled from countries, especially around the time of the **Crusades**. For example, in 1190, there was a massacre of Jews in the English city of York. People had accused the Jews of using the blood of Christian children in their religious rituals. A Christian mob responded by burning Jews who had taken refuge in a castle tower. One hundred years after the massacre in York, all Jews were expelled from England – a ban that lasted until 1656.

Jews were also blamed for the Black Death, a plague that killed approximately 60 per cent of people in Europe during the Middle Ages. At this time, Jews were also persecuted in Spain, where thousands of Jewish people were executed between 1066 and 1492, when Jews were expelled. This was followed by significant persecution of Jews in Russia, Germany and the Middle East in particular in the 1800s.

The yellow badge issued to Jews by the Nazi government in Germany from 1941 to 1945.

The Holocaust

The most severe persecution of Jews took place in the twentieth century. In 1933, Adolf Hitler and his political party, the Nazis, came to power in Germany. Living conditions in Germany were very poor at this time and Hitler blamed this on Jews. He said that they were enemies of Germany and he wanted to destroy them in what was called the Final Solution, the name given by the Nazis to the mass extermination of Jews. Jews were confined to small areas in cities called ghettos and then taken to concentration camps. There, they were executed, usually in gas

> 66 If heaven was full of paper and the oceans full of ink, I could not express my pain. 99
>
> A child survivor of Auschwitz, a concentration camp

chambers. The best-known concentration camp is Auschwitz, in Poland. It is estimated that six million of the nine million Jews living in Europe at the time were killed between 1933 and the end of the Second World War in 1945. This mass killing of Jewish people is usually known as the **Holocaust**. However, many Jews (and non-Jews) do not like this term because it originally referred to a burnt animal sacrifice. They use the word **Shoah**, which means calamity or catastrophe, instead.

Timeline of persecution in Nazi Germany

1935 – Signs forbidding Jews from swimming pools and public places are put up. The Nuremberg laws forbid Jews from voting or marrying a German and take away their German citizenship.

1939 – Jews are forced to live in ghettos and have their businesses taken away by the Nazis.

1942 – An event called the Wansee Conference finalises Nazi plans for the extermination of Jews in Europe.

1933 – Jewish business are boycotted; Jewish civil servants, lawyers and teachers lose their jobs. Schoolchildren are taught that Jews were racially inferior.

1938 – Jewish doctors are banned and Jewish children are banned from schools. On 9 and 10 November attacks on Jewish homes, businesses and synagogues take place. This event is called Kristallnacht (meaning 'Night of Broken Glass' in German).

1941 – Jews have to wear a star of David badge for identification. Many Jews in Russia are murdered by Nazi Einsatzgruppen ('task forces').

Anti-Semitism today

Anti-Semitism still exists in the UK and many other parts of the world today. It might take the form of online abuse, personal attacks or attacks on people's property. In the UK, a charity called the Campaign Against Anti-Semitism aims to educate people about anti-Semitism in the hope that it will be eliminated. Every year, on 27 January, Holocaust Memorial Day takes place so that people do not forget what happened.

Protestors in London challenging antisemitism by demanding zero-tolerance and greater action by the police and government.

Key vocabulary

anti-Semitism Persecution of Jewish people

Crusades A series of wars between Christians and Muslims

Holocaust The killing of six million Jews by Nazi Germany

persecution Discrimination against people because of their beliefs

Shoah Another term for the Holocaust, which means calamity or catastrophe

Check your understanding

1. What is meant by 'anti-Semitism'?
2. How were Jews persecuted in the Middle Ages?
3. How many Jews were killed in the Holocaust?
4. Create a timeline of Jewish persecution in Nazi Germany.
5. Does anti-Semitism still exist today?

Jewish responses to the Holocaust

Jews believe that God is all-powerful (omnipotent), all-loving (omnibenevolent) and all-knowing (omniscient). How does this present difficulties when considering issues such as the Holocaust?

The 'problem of evil'

Over the course of history, people have tried to understand how God and evil can both exist. If God knows everything, he knows evil exists. If God is all powerful, he has the power to stop evil. If God is all good, surely he wants to stop evil. The existence of evil suggests that either God does not exist, or that he is not all-loving, all-powerful and all-knowing. Since the Holocaust, Jews have thought and written much about this 'problem of evil'.

Richard Rubenstein

In 1960, a Jewish man called Richard Rubenstein wrote a book called *After Auschwitz*. In it he argued that after the horror of the Holocaust Jews could no longer believe that God is omnipotent, or that they are his chosen people. Rubenstein said that the covenant between God and Abraham had been destroyed. After the Holocaust, more Jews became secular Jews. They could not believe in God, but wanted to continue the practices and rituals of Judaism. Rubenstein still believed in God and did not think that people should become atheists, but he thought that God had no involvement in or impact on the world. He did think, though, that it was still valuable to live a Jewish life, because the rituals gave life meaning.

Richard Rubenstein.

Eliezer Berkovits

Eliezer Berkovits was an Orthodox Jewish rabbi who claimed that God was not responsible for the Holocaust. He argued that although God wanted to stop the suffering he could not do this without interfering with human **free will**. God had to allow extreme suffering and evil to happen because he had given freedom to human beings. Berkovits said that God had to 'hide his face' (**hester panim**) during the Holocaust. He argued that, rather than speaking about the absence of God during the Holocaust, people should consider the absence of humanity. Jews today should use their free will to have a renewed faith and desire to make the world a better and more peaceful place.

Emil Fackenheim

Emil Fackenheim was a rabbi who wrote in the 1940s. He argued that turning away from Judaism after the Holocaust was the equivalent of giving Hitler a victory – Hitler's aim had been to wipe Judaism from the face of the earth, and if Jews abandoned their religion then Hitler would have achieved his goal. Fackenheim claimed that Jews have a responsibility to unite and continue the Jewish family and faith. He said that this was the 614th mitzvah that Jews should follow.

Anne Frank

Anne Frank was a Jewish girl born in 1929. She and her family fled from Nazi Germany to Amsterdam in the Netherlands in order to avoid persecution. She and her family hid in an attic in Amsterdam for two years before being arrested and sent to a concentration camp, where she died of disease at the age of 15. While in hiding, she wrote a diary, which has since been translated into 67 languages and has sold over 30 million copies.

Who has allowed us to suffer so terribly up till now? It is God that has made us as we are, but it will be God, too, who will raise us up again. If we bear all this suffering and if there are still Jews left, when it is over, then Jews, instead of being doomed, will be held up as an example. Who knows, it might even be our religion from which the world and all peoples learn good, and for that reason and that reason alone do we have to suffer now.

Anne Frank

The Tanakh on suffering

The Tanakh does not give one clear explanation for why God allows suffering. The book of Job suggests that humans should not try to understand why some good people suffer. In this book, Job, the main character, is tested by God, who allows Satan to attack him. Job loses everything that is important to him, yet remains faithful to God. God blesses him with more than he had before as a reward for his loyalty.

Other traditional Jewish responses to the question of suffering include the idea that suffering is in some way beneficial and therefore not a bad thing. In the Tanakh, the prophet Isaiah is described as a *suffering servant*, and so some rabbis suggest that Jews suffer in order to pay for the wickedness of the rest of humanity.

Key vocabulary

free will The ability to choose how to act

hester panim The belief that God 'hid his face' during the Holocaust because he could not interfere with free will

Check your understanding

1. What is the 'problem of evil'?
2. How could the Tanakh help Jews understand why there is evil and suffering in the world?
3. Explain how one Jewish thinker responded to the Holocaust.
4. Who was Anne Frank and how did she try to understand the suffering of Jews during the Holocaust?
5. 'There is no satisfactory response to the problem of evil for Jews.' Discuss this statement.

Unit 2: Judaism in the modern world
What is Zionism?

How have Jews tried to create their own state and what difficulties have they faced?

At the end of the nineteenth century, Jews all over Europe were being persecuted. Some decided that the solution was to create their own Jewish state where they could practise their religion freely. This ambition was called **Zionism**. The Holocaust (see pages 38–39) led many Jews to believe that having their own land was not only desirable but necessary for the survival of the Jewish people.

Zionists thought about where they could establish their homeland and decided that they should return to Jerusalem and the area surrounding it. Their ancestors had fled from this region 2000 years earlier in order to avoid persecution from their Roman rulers. During their reign, the Romans changed the name of the area from Judea to Palestine.

The battle for land

Over the course of history, Jerusalem has had many rulers, including Jews, Christians and Muslims. In 1917, during the First World War, Britain captured Jerusalem from the Muslim Ottoman Empire, which had ruled the area for 400 years. The British government supported the idea of establishing a Jewish state in Palestine, and hundreds of thousands of Jews moved there. However, this caused great difficulties between the Jews and the **Palestinians** who were already living there.

In 1947, war broke out between the Jews and Palestinians, and in 1948 the **United Nations** (UN) decided to split Jerusalem in two. The eastern half was given to Jordan and the western half became part of the **State of Israel**, which was the first Jewish state to exist for 2000 years. This decision was controversial because neither side thought that the other should exist as a nation or rule over part of Jerusalem. Jerusalem was home to Jewish people's ancestors and was the location of the Temple, so it was very important. However, the city is also important for Muslims – it is the location of the Al-Aqsa Mosque and the Dome of the Rock, which, according to the Qur'an, is where the Prophet Muhammad ascended to the heavens from earth during an event called the Night Journey.

During the Six-Day War in 1967, the Jewish **Israelis** captured more land from the Jordanians, including eastern Jerusalem and a Palestinian area called the West Bank. Since then, violence between Israeli Jews and Palestinian Muslims has continued to escalate and attempts to create lasting peace have been unsuccessful. In 2007, an area of land called the

Date	Ruler
3150 BCE	Cananites
1006 BCE	Israelites (Jewish)
586 BCE	Hellenists (Greek)
37 BCE	Romans
348 AD	Byzantines (Christian)
638 AD	Early Muslim conquests
1099 AD	Crusaders (Christian)
1187 AD	Mamelukes and Ottomans
1917 AD	British (Christian)
1948 AD	State of Israel (Jewish)
Present	

This chart shows who ruled Jerusalem at various points in its history.

This map shows Israel and the surrounding area, with Jewish and Islamic areas highlighted.

Gaza Strip was returned to the Palestinians in an effort to improve the situation.

Israel today

Israel is a well-developed country with a population of about eight million people – 75 per cent of them are Jewish, 20 per cent are Muslim and five per cent are of other or no faith. This makes it the only place in the world with a majority Jewish population. Hebrew is the main language spoken. The capital is officially Jerusalem, though this is not recognised by many other countries. This is because they do not agree with the borders that Israel has put in place, which do not match the agreements made with the United Nations.

Anti-Zionist or anti-Semitic?

Anti-Zionism and anti-Semitism are not the same thing. Anti-Zionism means opposition to the existence of the Jewish state of Israel while anti-Semitism means hostility towards and prejudice against Jewish people. Some people argue that it is impossible to separate criticism of Zionism or Israeli politics from criticism of Judaism itself. Some even say that labelling someone a 'Zionist' is a form of abuse. Others claim that the Israeli government and its supporters deliberately confuse the definitions of Judaism with Zionism to try and stop people criticising their political decisions.

Key vocabulary

Israelis People who live in Israel; mainly Jewish

Palestinians People who live in and around the State of Israel; mainly Muslims

State of Israel A Jewish state set up by the United Nations in 1948, which has since expanded

United Nations An organisation set up after the Second World War to keep world peace

Zionism A Jewish movement that originally aimed to establish, and now aims to continue, the Jewish state of Israel

Controversy within Judaism

Zionism has always been a controversial issue within Judaism. A Holocaust survivor called Rabbi Joel Teitelbaum believed that Jews should wait for the Messiah to return them to the Promised Land and then set up a religious society there. He claimed that the Holocaust was God's punishment of the Jews for not waiting for the Messiah. Another Jewish thinker, Menachem Hartom, argued the opposite. He thought that the Holocaust was a punishment because Jews had fitted in to other cultures and not returned to the land God had given them. For other Jews, any suggestion that the Holocaust was God's punishment is seen as offensive. Former Chief Rabbi Jonathan Sacks wrote:

More than a million children were gassed, burned, shot, tortured or buried alive … God forbid that we should add to their death the sin of saying that it was justified.

Jonathan Sacks, *Crisis and Covenant: Jewish Thought After the Holocaust* (Manchester University Press, 1992), p. 32

Check your understanding

1 Why did Jews want a country that could become their 'homeland'?

2 Why were the events of 1948 and 1967 controversial?

3 Describe what the country of Israel is like today.

4 Why might someone say that Zionism is an unhelpful term?

5 Explain why Zionism has been controversial within Judaism.

Unit 2: Judaism in the modern world
Knowledge organiser

Key facts

- Jews observe a day of rest each week, called Shabbat or the Sabbath. This is a day of rest on which they are not allowed to do any work.

- On Shabbat, many Jews will go to services at the synagogue. They also enjoy a special meal with family in which certain rituals are performed.

- The main Jewish festivals are Rosh Hashanah (the first day of the Jewish new year), Yom Kippur (the Day of Atonement) and Pesach (Passover).

- Jews observe certain rituals at significant moments in their lives. In ancient times, when a child was born, the mother would have to stay away from the Temple for 40 days for a boy and 80 days for a girl.

- Circumcision is a ritual in which a male's foreskin is removed, in remembrance of God's covenant with Abraham. This takes place when a boy is eight days old.

- Bar Mitzvah and Bat Mitzvah are ceremonies that mark a boy's or a girl's 'coming of age' at 13 years old. They must study carefully for these ceremonies and afterwards are considered to be responsible for their own actions and faith.

- The Jewish marriage is in two parts: the engagement and the full marriage. The ceremony is led by a rabbi who, along with the guests, recites the seven blessings for the couple.

- Jews are usually buried rather than cremated. Burial takes place within 24 hours of death if possible, and someone stays with the body the whole time until the burial.

- There are three stages to mourning after someone dies: Aninut, Shivah and Sheloshim. If a parent has died, there are two additional stages: Yud Bet Chodesh and Yahrzeit.

- Jewish law states that human life is sacred. Jews are allowed to break some of their laws if doing so will save someone's life. This principle is known as Pikuach Nefesh.

- Jews have been persecuted since ancient times. They have been expelled from countries where they were living many times, including from England in the 1200s.

- The worst case of Jewish persecution was at the hands of the German Nazis from 1933 to 1945. Millions of Jews were sent to concentration camps, where they were executed. This is known as the Holocaust or Shoah.

- The 'problem of evil' is the question of how God can allow terrible things such as the Holocaust to happen. If he is all-loving, all-powerful and all-knowing, he would prevent these events. Jews have different interpretations of and responses to the problem of evil.

- Zionism is a movement of re-establishment and development of a Jewish homeland in the area around Jerusalem. After the Second World War, Jews were allowed to return to Palestine, but this caused great conflict with the Palestinian people who were already living there. Difficulties continue in the region today, as Jewish Israelis and Muslim Palestinians both consider the region to be their homeland.

Key vocabulary

anti-Semitism Persecution of Jewish people

atheist Someone who does not believe in God

Bar Mitzvah A ceremony for boys at the age of 13; it literally means 'son of the commandments'

Bat Mitzvah A ceremony for girls at the age of 12 or 13; it literally means 'daughter of the commandments'

Crusades A series of wars between Christians and Muslims

eulogy A speech given in praise of someone who has just died

free will The ability to choose how to act

Gehinnom A place of purification in the afterlife

hester panim The belief that God 'hid his face' during the Holocaust because he could not interfere with free will

Holocaust The killing of six million Jews by Nazi Germany

huppah A canopy which a couple stand under during their marriage ceremony to represent starting a new home together

Israelis People who live in Israel; mainly Jewish

mohel Someone who is both medically and religiously qualified to perform a circumcision

Palestinians People who live in and around the State of Israel; mainly Muslims

persecution Discrimination against people because of their beliefs

Pikuach Nefesh The principle that nearly any religious law can be broken in order to preserve human life

pogrom An attack on Jews

Seder meal A symbolic meal eaten at Pesach

seven blessings Blessings recited by the rabbi and others at a wedding ceremony

Shabbat/Sabbath A day of rest and religious observance

Shoah Another term for the Holocaust, which means calamity or catastrophe

State of Israel A Jewish state set up by the United Nations in 1948, which has since expanded

United Nations An organisation set up after the Second World War to keep world peace

Zionism A Jewish movement originally aimed to establish, and now aims to continue, the Jewish state of Israel

Key people

Eliezer Berkovits A rabbi who believed that God had to hide his face (hester panim) during the Holocaust so as not to interfere with human free will

Emil Fackenheim A rabbi who thought that the 614th mitzvah Jews should follow after the Holocaust was to unite and continue the Jewish family and faith so that Hitler did not win

Anne Frank A Jewish girl who wrote a diary while in hiding during the Holocaust

Richard Rubenstein A Jewish writer who claimed that Jews cannot think of God as omnipotent or that they are his chosen people after the Holocaust

A Jewish family at Shabbat.

Index

Acknowledgements

Every effort has been made to trace copyright holders and to obtain their permission for the use of copyright material.

The publishers will gladly receive any information enabling them to rectify any error or omission at the first opportunity.

The publishers would like to thank the following for permission to reproduce copyright material:

(t = top, b = bottom, c = centre, l = left, r = right)

Text

p41 Anne Frank – 'THE DIARY OF A YOUNG GIRL: THE DEFINITIVE EDITION by Anne Frank, edited by Otto H Frank and Mirjam Pressler, translated by Susan Massotty (Viking, 1997) copyright © The Anne Frank-Fonds, Basle, Switzerland, 1991. English translation copyright © Doubleday a division of Bantam Doubleday Dell Publishing Group Inc, 1995.

Photographs

Cover and title page bogdan ionescu/Shutterstock, pp6–7 Yadid Levy/Alamy Stock Photo, p9 mikhail/Shutterstock, p10 Lebrecht Music&Arts Photo Library/Alamy Stock Photo, p11 Prisma Archivo/Alamy Stock Photo, p12 DEA/A/Dagli orti/Getty Images, p13 Karol Koziowski/Shutterstock, p14 t Zvonimir Atletic/Shutterstock, p14 b robertharding/Alamy Stock Photo, p15 paul prescott/Shutterstock. Inc, p16 Matt Ragen/Shutterstock, p17 t robertharding/Alamy Stock Photo, p17 b Culture Club/Getty Images, p18 ChameleonsEye/Shutterstock, p19 TravelCollection/Alamy Stock Photo, p20 railway fx/Shutterstock, p21 Scythian/Shutterstock, p22 t Kobby Dagan/Shutterstock, p22 b imageBroker/Alamy Stock Photo, p23 t david156/Shutterstock, p23 b Anneka/Shutterstock, p25 dominique landau/Shutterstock, pp26–27 Zoonar GmbH/Alamy Stock Photo, p28 PhotoAlto sas/Alamy Stock Photo, p29 t S1001/Shutterstock, p29 b Robert Gray/Alamy Stock Photo, p30 Gregory Gerber/Shutterstock, p31 t ChameleonsEye/Shutterstock, p31 c Madlen/Shutterstock, p31 b supercat/Shutterstock, p32 ChameleonsEye/Shutterstock, p33 Rodolfo Arpia/Alamy Stock Photo, p34 t Robert Mulder/Alamy Stock Photo, p34 b a katz/Shutterstock, p35 Ira Berger/Alamy Stock Photo, p36 RosaireneBetancourt 9/Alamy Stock Photo, p37 Jack Guez/AFP/Getty Images, p38 t Lanmas/Alamy Stock Photo, p38 b Galerie Bilderwelt/Getty Images, p39 Campaign Against Antisemitism, p40 t Sean Gallup/Getty Images, p40 b American Jewish Archive, p41 Pictorial Press Ltd/Alamy Stock Photo, p45 ASAP/Alamy Stock Photo.